JUBILEE

T0331529

Chris Goode

JUBILEE

from the original screenplay by
Derek Jarman & James Whaley

with additional material by the Company

OBERON BOOKS
LONDON

WWW.OBERONBOOKS.COM

This adaptation first published in 2017 by Oberon Books Ltd
521 Caledonian Road, London N7 9RH
Tel: +44 (0) 20 7607 3637 / Fax: +44 (0) 20 7607 3629
e-mail: info@oberonbooks.com
www.oberonbooks.com

Jubilee copyright © Derek Jarman and James Whaley, 1978

Adaptation copyright © Chris Goode, 2017

Reprinted with revisions in 2018

Lyrics from 'I Want to Be Free' reprinted by permission of First Night Records. All rights reserved.

Chris Goode is hereby identified as author of this adaptation in accordance with section 77 of the Copyright, Designs and Patents Act 1988. The author has asserted their moral rights.

All rights whatsoever in this play are strictly reserved and application for performance etc. should be made before commencement of rehearsal to Chris Goode c/o Oberon Books. No performance may be given unless a licence has been obtained, and no alterations may be made in the title or the text of the play without the author's prior written consent.

You may not copy, store, distribute, transmit, reproduce or otherwise make available this publication (or any part of it) in any form, or binding or by any means (print, electronic, digital, optical, mechanical, photocopying, recording or otherwise), without the prior written permission of the publisher. Any person who does any unauthorized act in relation to this publication may be liable to criminal prosecution and civil claims for damages.

A catalogue record for this book is available from the British Library.

PB ISBN: 9781786823885
E ISBN: 9781786823892

Cover image: Gu Photography.

Visit www.oberonbooks.com to read more about all our books and to buy them. You will also find features, author interviews and news of any author events, and you can sign up for e-newsletters so that you're always first to hear about our new releases.

'We are smashing up the present because we come from the future.'

– Greek anarchist slogan

Characters

ELIZABETH I

The Virgin Queen, Astraea, paradigm of royalty

JOHN DEE

Court astrologer, alchemist and magician to Elizabeth I

ARIEL

Angel, mercurial messenger, glitter punk, scintilla

BOD

Boadicea, Anybody, Queen of the new age.
Anithesis of Elizabeth

AMYL

Historian of the void

MAD

Revolutionary and pyromaniac

CRABS

Lovelorn but sexed-up, a casualty of true romance

VIV

a.k.a. Viva, radical performance artist, sympathetic,
a little broken

ANGEL & SPHINX

Incestuous brothers, Queer As Fuck

KID

A teen with raw talent, just waiting to be discovered

BORGIA GINZ

Malevolent impresario and media mogul

MAX
Mercenary and plastic horticulturalist

HAPPY DAYS
Rock'n'roll throwback lothario

LOUNGE LIZARD
Sham pop phenomenon

WAITRESS at the Kaos Cafe

SCHMITZER
Borgia's personal assistant

TWO COPS

TWO WAITERS at Borgia's country house

COMPERE of the Seal Club

ASSORTED REVELLERS at the Seal Club

A DOG, or a man who wants to be treated as one

A RHINOCEROS

VOICE, most probably the Ghost of Heathcote Williams

THE DIRECTOR'S VOICE, hardly intelligible

Jubilee premiered at the Royal Exchange Theatre, Manchester, on 2 November 2017. Cast and crew were as follows:

QUEEN ELIZABETH I	Toyah Willcox
JOHN DEE/BORGIA GINZ/	
WAITRESS/COP #1	Harold Finley
ARIEL/VIV	Lucy Ellinson
BOD	Sophie Stone
AMYL	Travis Alabanza
MAD/MAX	Temi Wilkey
CRABS	Rose Wardlaw
ANGEL/SCHMITZER	Tom Ross-Williams
SPHINX/RHINOCEROS	Craig Hamilton
KID	Yandass Ndlovu
HAPPY DAYS/LOUNGE LIZARD/	
COP #2/DOG/COMPERE	Gareth Kieran Jones

ENSEMBLE: Lauren Greer, Billie Meredith, Gaynor Isherwood, Karl Olsen, Vincent Dugdale, Chris Sampson, Ross Fitzgerald, Rose Walker, Clare McNulty, Oceana Cage, Alan Maguire, Emma Campbell, Katy Preen, Madeleine Healey, Keri Sparkes, Wensday Pain, Maria Theodorou

Director	Chris Goode
Designer	Chloe Lamford
Lighting Designer	Lee Curran
Sound Designer	Timothy X Atack
Movement Director	Sasha Milavic Davies
Fight Director	Alison de Burgh
Associate Director	Atri Banerjee
Contributing Artists	Angela Clerkin, Griffyn Gilligan,
	Ira Brand, Kamal Kaan
Critical Writer	Maddy Costa

'Rule Britannia' and 'I Want To Be Free' specially recorded by The Go! Team

Stage Manager	Harriet Stewart
Deputy Stage Manager	Rosie Giarratana
Assistant Stage Manager	Sophie Keers
Sign Language Interpreters	Sarah Glendenning,
	Siobhan Rocks,
	Andrea Scott,
	Ruth Andrews

PART 1

0. PRE-SHOW

A dimly lit squat, known to its inhabitants as H.Q. A chaotic landscape of necessary junk. No one home.

In the centre of the space, QUEEN ELIZABETH sits at an outsize dressing table. Candle light; numerous mirrors multiply the candles. A skull. Various artefacts. A touch of Rembrandt about the composition. The QUEEN is applying the last of her make-up, her costume, etc. – painstakingly assembling her identity.

DR DEE watches her protectively from the shadows.

1.

DR DEE spies a Dansette-style record player amid the bric-a-brac of H.Q., with a pile of punk records next to it, classic and contemporary, interspersed with the occasional charity shop treasure – ironic easy listening or marginal 80's pop. He looks through the records, selects one, takes the disc out of its sleeve, puts it on the turntable, sets it playing. It is a sound effects record: English sea birds, wind, waves, a coastal ambience.

For now, ELIZABETH does not notice DEE's presence, or the sound coming from the record player.

Floating above the coastal sounds, we hear the words of Rilke in intimate voiceover – the ghost of Heathcote Williams, probably…

VOICE: Who if I cried would hear me among the angelic
orders? And even if one of them suddenly
pressed me against his heart, I should fade in the strength
of his stronger existence. For beauty's nothing
but the begininng of Terror we're still just able to bear,
and why we adore it so is because it serenely
disdains to destroy us.

A roll of distant thunder. For the first time, QUEEN ELIZABETH notices the presence of DEE.

ELIZABETH: John Dee, some pretty distractions, which you call angels, call forth to forget our cares.

JOHN DEE: Your Majesty, as once a virgin fashioned the whole earth, so by a virgin it shall have rebirth. So says the old sage wisdom.

ELIZABETH: Dear our own Dr John, our triumphant antinomy, our kingdom's eyes, it pleaseth me to see and have discourse with angels.

DEE takes his staff and points it to the four corners of the compass as he speaks.

JOHN DEE: Your Majesty, this spell we cast in the name of Christ Jesus and his Angelic hosts, calling forth a fiery spiritual creature: our angel, Ariel. – Metatron! Angel commander! I cast for Ariel, pearl of fire, my only star. Send forth my flower, my green herb.

The smoke and ashes of the past, which hang like morning mist in veils across the universe, now part in swirls and eddies, and through them, my star, my angel Ariel flies with mirrored eyes, leaving a sparkling phosphorescent trail across the universe. Down, down he plummets towards earth, through the great vacuum, on the curve of infinity – like a fiery rose he descends!

A sudden burst of radiant light as ARIEL materialises aloft. Thunderclap. QUEEN ELIZABETH is frightened. She shields her eyes against the light.

A bed of etheral music, out-of-focus movement within it.

ARIEL: All hail, great master! grave sir, hail! I come
To answer thy best pleasure; be't to fly,
To swim, to dive into the fire, to ride
On the curl'd clouds, to thy strong bidding task
Ariel and all his quality.

ELIZABETH: This vision far exceedeth all expectation. Such an abstract never before I spied!

JOHN DEE: An angel, your Majesty, is the sun's true shadow. – Spirit Ariel! Her Majesty seeks to have knowledge, to swim in those pure waters that are the essence which binds all creation.

The music is starting to come into focus.

ARIEL: By me this task shall be performed, for I am that pure and clarified spirit by which thou may'st turn all metals into gold. Sweet Majesty, pluck up thy heart and be merry, for I shall reveal to thee the shadow of this time.

The music suddenly coalesces, revealing itself as the huge guitar riff from 'Two Librans' by The Fall. Overlaid with sounds of gunfire, aerial bombardment, all-out war...

The lights go on throughout H.Q.

Despite the loudness of the music we can just make out the DIRECTOR'S voice in v/o:

DIRECTOR: And cue Temi.

A sudden influx of figures – some of the inhabitants of the squat:

MAD comes first, carrying a machine gun. She has fun threatening the audience, always with a grin of pleasure. Bouncing off the walls already, thrilled by the chaos that builds around her.

ANGEL and SPHINX, pushing CRABS in a shopping trolley. CRABS is delighting in being pushed around. She wears Audrey Hepburn sunglasses, sucks Lolita-like on a Chupa Chup, flips through a high-end fashion magazine full of pictures of pretty boys.

ANGEL and SPHINX desert CRABS and her trolley. They can't keep their hands off each other a moment longer. They kiss wildly and tear at each others' clothes, until in no time at all they are both naked and making out passionately on a dirty mattress on the floor. Lots of love and laughter.

Finally, AMYL comes just a little way into the space. She is pushing an old-fashioned pram which is on fire. MAD is delighted and intercepts the pram. She wheels it around while AMYL smiles at the mayhem, still lurking on the edge of the room. Eventually, MAD wheels the flaming pram away.

A DOG – or is it just some random guy in dog fetish gear? – runs into the room and excitedly scampers round and round, barking at everything and everyone.

Throughout all this, DR DEE is escorting QUEEN ELIZABETH to a place of greater safety: a provisional royal box to which ARIEL is still putting the finishing touches as the QUEEN is led up the stairs. A throne-like chair surrounded by yet more junk – dismembered mannequins, half-destroyed placards from forgotten demonstrations, a heap of old sweating binbags…

Two stage hands dressed in black bloc gear wheel out the QUEEN's dressing table. The DOG runs round their legs and tries to bite them / lick them / hump them, depending on his mood. He leaves with them.

AMYL picks a spray can off the floor and adds some new graffiti to one of the walls, which are already covered with militant queer slogans and manifesto fragments.

CRABS gets out of her trolley and finds an old sofa or mattress to recline on where she can continue to look through her magazine.

The music ends.

2.

MAD, toting her gun, addresses the audience.

MAD: All right, you motherfuckers, listen up. We are proud to welcome to these esteemed headquarters a person I just know you're going to love. She's going to start this shit-show off with a little history lesson. I give you England's last remaining hope and glory: Miss Amyl Nitrate, come on down!

AMYL steps forward into the light. Cheesey glamorous showbiz music.

MAD goes to the mic to introduce AMYL and her outfit.

MAD: Tonight, as you can see, Miss Nitrate is favouring us with an outfit conceived in the fathomless dreams of a car-crash victim in a persistent vegetative state. Her pastel twinset is from a leading London charity shop, namely the People's Dispensary for Sick Animals, who supply so much of her low couture because God knows she's made more animals sick than anyone else around here. The pearls belonged to her late grandmother, and one has to assume she thinks it was worth all that digging to get at them. Her make-up is inspired by some of the most distressing casualties of the First World War, and her hair is by Kensington and Chelsea Borough Council.

AMYL: Fuck off.

The music ends abruptly.

MAD: The language they teach you in finishing school these days! The point is: there are, in the words of the once and future song, no more heroes any more. Just empty suits inflated by the Fake News Media, right? SAD. But in a world without heroes, Amyl Nitrate is someone we can all believe in. She's the real thing – and I don't mean Coke, suckers. So, enough from me: heeeere's Amyl! *(Singling out someone – ideally a young person – in the audience.)* Fucking pay attention!

MAD hurls herself down on a beaten up sofa and picks up a dog-eared old issue of Hit-Girl to read.

AMYL sits down demurely at a desk on which are placed: a globe – some regions of which have been blacked out or otherwise attacked and defaced; a souvenir shop-style Union Jack flag propped up in an empty jam jar; a fragrance bottle (Cefiro by Floris); a glass milk bottle half-filled with water, and a heavy tumbler. A beaten up old MacBook covered in stickers and slogans sits open towards her, glowing weakly.

AMYL: Good evening, everyone. How nice to be with you. One gets a much better class of audience at the subsidised theatre, I must say. The cinema is full of scumbags. Eating their pick-'n'-mix and live-tweeting their inane thoughts to their seven followers. Ugh. Thank you for your bourgeois stultification, it makes for a much nicer atmosphere.

So, welcome to *Jubilee*. An iconic film most of you have never even heard of, adapted by an Oxbridge twat for a dying medium, spoiled by millennials, ruined by diversity, and constantly threatening to go all interactive. You poor fuckers. Well, don't worry. There's really no audience participation in this thing. I didn't train my arse off for all those years only to get to the Royal Exchange and randomly decide to turn the spotlight away from me and onto some old white middle-class cunt accountant in M&S comfort-waist chinos. So you can relax…Well, maybe not relax exactly.

But I mean really: what is the point of doing plays? And films? And…installations? If you live with integrity, art is totally redundant. Our school motto was: 'Make your desires reality'. No fucking chance of that if you're a queer little kid like I was, with such dangerous desires. So you fall back on fantasy. I lost myself in school plays and fan fiction and idiot pop music.

But when you start to live in a way that your desires really do become reality, you don't need fantasy any more. You don't need any more art.

She pauses and pours herself a glass of water from the milk bottle.

I was so lucky. When I was fifteen I saw one of those Channel 5 documentaries. The 100 Most Evil Women dot dot dot Ever. This glamorous parade of serial killers and child torturers and stone-cold sadists. The narrator said their crimes were unimaginable. Oh please! That just shows the poverty of your imagination.

Inspired by these world-class bitches I started to live more and more intensely as myself. And as I did so, I became ever more fascinated by history. The stories we tell about who we all are, and who we're becoming. As you know there are no facts any more. For every fact there's an alternative fact. So it's all collapsed. You can put facts together any way you like. The good guys and the bad guys? It's all negotiable.

In 1992 a book was published called *The End of History*. That's how it felt back then, I suppose. History was over, politics was over, ideology was over. Capitalism had won. Neoliberalism had won. The West had won.

What happened next, kids?…Well?

The war in Bosnia. Genocide in Rwanda. The rise of the Taliban. Tony fucking Blair. Fucking Google. The war in Kosovo. George W. fucking Bush. 9/11. The war on abstract concepts. The Crusades part II. 170 people dead in a theatre in Moscow – you all should be so fucking lucky. 7/7. 2008: capitalism burns down, but it's OK, because you're all obsessed with some fat old journalist on fucking *Strictly*. Barack Obama, that murderous conman. The war in Gaza, episode whatever. David fucking Cameron. Deepwater Horizon. The Arab Spring, remember that? Syria. Occupy. 'The riots.' ISIS. ISIS. ISIS. Brexit. Trump. ISIS. Syria. Jeremy fucking Corbyn. The sad death of Sir Brucie Bonus.

A fuck of a lot has happened since the end of history. That's why I've started writing it all down. *(She gestures towards the MacBook.)* This lot take the piss but they're all fascinated. Course they are.

There's this old saying. Go outside, pick up the biggest rock you can find, drop it on your foot. Guess what? The past didn't go anywhere.

But here's my thing. Why drop the rock of history on your own foot, when you can use it to smash someone's head in?

Anyway, I'd better introduce you.

That's Mad over there. Short for Madeleine or Madonna or Mad Cow Disease, depending on who you ask. She calls herself a revolutionary pyromaniac. We just call her a maniac. She's my best mate so naturally I hate her guts.

And there's Crabs. I assume that's not her real name but I've never heard her called anything else. She's what would have been called, back in the 70s, a nympho. But of course we're more enlightened now so we prefer to use the phrase 'sex positive'. And believe me, even in these dark days, she remains strenuously positive.

The boys on the bed are Sphinx and Angel. Lovers, as you'll have already observed. Also: brothers. That's right, comrades, we're spending Arts Council money promoting incest. They're exceedingly sex positive too but no one fucking says that about boys. Do they, dear?

And then somewhere around here is Bod. Short for Bodicea or Are You Beach Body Ready? or who the fuck knows. Bod is queen of all she surveys. Our malignant dictator. Long to reign over us. She's our Head of State and, as you can see, we are in quite a state. Oh! Wait! Hark, I think I hear her now...

BOD breaks into the royal box. She grabs QUEEN ELIZABETH from behind and holds a flick-knife to her throat.

BOD: All right, you virgin bitch. I'm taking this.

BOD snatches the QUEEN's crown and runs off with it.

AMYL: So there you go, boys and girls. You've met the gang. And for the purposes of tonight's fiction, we all live here together in this squat. Is it utopia? Is it a dystopia? Frankly I've no idea how the fuck you expect to be able to tell the difference any more. Life in England right now is just about as degraded as it gets, but of course, as dear Mr Winston Churchill taught us, we keep buggering on. During a mass lobotomization programme a few years ago, most people in this country had their entire personalities removed and replaced with a set of wipeable coasters that say KEEP CALM AND CARRY ON. And so that's what we do. We Carry On Camping. As George Orwell wrote: if you want a vision of the present, imagine Barbara Windsor's bikini top accidentally popping off forever.

Well at least there's still Cefiro from Floris. Not all the good things have disappeared.

AMYL sprays herself with the fragrance.

The doorbell rings.

MAD: Oh, who's that?

AMYL: Don't look at me, I'm not getting it. I'm exhausted from my monologue.

MAD: Angel, you go. The exercise will do you good.

ANGEL: Fuck off.

MAD: You fuck off.

ANGEL gets off the bed and goes over to the door. MAD approaches the bed.

MAD: ...and while your back's turned I can have a go on your brother.

SPHINX: Don't think so, thanks.

ANGEL lets BOD in. She comes into the room, clutching a Lidl bag with something inside.

ANGEL: Here comes Bod.

BOD: Shut your eyes. All of you!...I said, shut your eyes, Angel.

She runs half way up the stairs, takes QUEEN ELIZABETH's crown out of the carrier bag and places it on her head.

BOD: All right, you can open them.

She mimes gunning them all down as they take in the spectacle of her new headgear.

SPHINX: Bloody hell! Where'd you get that from?

BOD: I captured it on manoeuvres. It's high fashion, darling.

SPHINX comes over, still naked; he takes the Lidl bag from BOD and puts it over his own head.

CRABS: Unexpected item in the bagging area.

MAD: I like it. I think it works.

3.

KID is busking in town – performing for small change.

KID: Thank you. Thanks very much. Um, if you're enjoying what I'm doing, maybe just put a little bit of money in the hat there? Anyone?

Okay well the next one I'm going to do is brand new, I only finished writing it, like, last night. So I hope I don't forget it.

She introduces and performs her newest song.

4.

AMYL has left her MacBook unattended on the desk. MAD takes the opportunity to take a look at the document she's been working on. She reads it aloud to the room.

MAD: History for Dummies by Amyl Nitrate.

AMYL: Leave it.

MAD: I think it's time your great work was shared with the world, don't you?

(Reads.) 'Chapter One. The History of England. It all began with William the Conqueror, who fucked over the Anglo-Saxons, carving the land into theirs and ours. The rich lived in mansions and ate beef from fat tables, while the poor were minding the cows on a bowl of porridge and got pushed around by these arrogant upstart foreigners.

'At first these two sides co-existed peaceably enough, meeting only on the racetrack and the battlefield, where they were united in fighting the rest of the world, whom they despised even more than they hated each other.

'But one day when there was no-one left to fight, they started to realise that the real enemy was at home, and that they should fight among themselves: the fancy cosmopolitan elite in their bubble, and the sons of the soil in all their ignorance and cowshit. At first they tried to slog it out with money, but then they realised it wasn't worth the paper it was written on, and so they had to fight with guns instead. The rest of the world heaved a huge sigh of relief to be rid of them and got on with their own business, and England slowly sank into the sea.'

Who are you writing this crap for, Amyl?

AMYL: Darling, everything I do, I do for myself. When I'm not making history, I write it. I try to condense it. Wouldn't it be great if all of history could be written on the surface of a Cipramil?

MAD: That's not how you deal with history, Amyl.

AMYL: All right. If you don't like it, why don't you write something.

5.

QUEEN ELIZABETH has been watching all of this from the royal box. Separately, ARIEL, who carries a hand mirror.

ARIEL: A thing that is infinite and eternal has no qualities, and in it, thinking and being cease to exist; it is everything and nothing. Every seeming fixed and certain thing is only relative; that alone is fixed and certain which is subject to change.

Yaasss, Queen: I am the mirror, the consuming fire. Mine is the power which will summon back the sun: stealing the great light itself, so in thy darkness thou may'st see.

ARIEL vanishes. The QUEEN is startled and afraid.

6.

The KAOS Cafe – a knowingly retro greasy spoon cafe.

CRABS and KID sitting together, the only customers for now. A bored WAITRESS in a blonde wig regards her own reflection in a hand mirror, fixing her lipstick.

CRABS has bought breakfast for KID, while she herself sucks on a lollipop.

CRABS: What did you say your name was again?

KID: Kid.

CRABS: How were your eggs?

KID: Good thanks.

CRABS: Do you want some more?

KID: No thank you. Thanks very much.

CRABS: That's all right, hon. You're very talented you know.

KID: Thank you.

CRABS: What do you do? Are you a student?

KID: No I dropped out. I wanted to concentrate full-time on my music.

CRABS: Yeah I got kicked out of college too. Who cares. It's for arseholes. You're gorgeous, you know that?

KID: Thank you.

CRABS: You really are. You know who I should introduce you to? Have you ever heard of Borgia Ginz?

KID: *(Shakes her head.)*

CRABS: He's like the number one impresario in the business.

KID: *(Looks blank.)*

CRABS: Like a manager. He's always on the look-out for fresh young talent. Just like you. He's an extremely powerful man. He practically owns the media. He and I go way back. Long story. My name's Crabs, by the way. I'm an actress.

KID: Have you been in any films?

CRABS: ...I've mostly been concentrating on theatre lately. Devising.

KID: *(Looks blank again.)*

CRABS: I'm a devotee of Lecoq.

KID: Oh.

> *The conversation is interrupted by the arrival of BOD and MAD. CRABS is not pleased.*

BOD: Tea please! Hello Crabs. Fancy seeing you here.

CRABS: Amyl not with you?

MAD: No, she's much too busy with her magnum opus.

CRABS: Oh what a shame.

KID: *(Politely, to BOD, holding out her hand.)* Hello, I'm Kid…My dad's got a suit like that.

BOD is unimpressed. She walks away.

CRABS: That's Bod.

MAD: She's royalty.

KID: Oh!

CRABS: She's touchy about that suit. There's a story behind it.

MAD: You don't say.

CRABS: She hooked up with this super-shady Russian oligarch at a party. He takes her back to the Dorchester where he was staying, and fucks her, rather inadequately. He squirts, turns over, starts snoring. She hates that more than anything. So she decides to nick his clothes. She gets dressed in the dark and makes her escape. Half way home she finds five thousand quid in unused fifties in the inside pocket. So now she wears it for luck.

MAD: Two years you've been telling that story. I'm still not sure it's true. The only thing Crabs loves more than a good sex story is a bad sex story. She's fucking obsessed. Literally.

CRABS: I'm a very sexual person. What's wrong with that?

MAD: Don't get me started.

CRABS: You fuck Bod.

MAD: That's not fucking. That's unarmed combat. With the occasional happy ending.

ANGEL, SPHINX and VIV are arriving.

CRABS: Here come the reinforcements.

VIV: Hi Crabs. Who's your friend?

CRABS: *(Hesitates.)*

SPHINX: Don't worry, mate, she's not going to steal her away from you. She's got me and Angel to keep her occupied.

VIV: I don't need to be kept occupied! Jesus, you sound like bloody property guardians. *(To KID.)* Hello, I'm Viv. This is Sphinx, and Angel.

KID: I'm Kid.

BOD: *(Suddenly.)* WHERE'S MY FUCKING TEA?

WAITRESS: Right! I'm not having that sort of language in my cafe. Get out, you! All of you! Bunch of louts!

ANGEL: We only just got here!

WAITRESS: You're all together! *(Gesturing to CRABS.)* And she never bought anything first or last!

CRABS: I bought her breakfast actually!

KID: That's true! I'm the one who never bought anything.

BOD: Some of us are trying to get served!

MAD: This place is a shithole. *(She starts flicking her lighter.)*

ANGEL: Uh oh. She's off.

MAD grabs the WAITRESS from behind. BOD pulls out her flick-knife and holds it to the WAITRESS's neck.

VIV: Right, I'm out.

SPHINX: Bloody hell, this escalated quickly. Come on bruv.

VIV, ANGEL and SPHINX make a quick break for it.

BOD: *(To the WAITRESS.)* Listen, Resting Bitch Face: when I order tea I want tea. Not being ignored. Not being yelled at. Just tea. If you read your fucking job description, it won't be far down the list.

MAD: She needs to be taught a lesson, Bod.

WAITRESS: No! Please!

MAD pulls the WAITRESS's wig off and puts it on herself.

MAD: It's like this. If your house is ugly then burn it. If the street you live in makes you depressed then bulldoze it. And if the fucking cook can't fucking cook, or won't fucking cook, then you kill her. Right?

After a moment's hesitation with her knife still pressed up against the WAITRESS's neck, BOD grabs the nearest squeezy ketchup dispenser and squirts ketchup all over the WAITRESS.

BOD: There, that's better.

She throws the sobbing WAITRESS to the floor.

MAD: Fuck me, I thought you were actually going to kill her then.

BOD: Nah. Welcome to theatre, babes. Everything's fake.

7.

We hear JOHN DEE in voiceover:

JOHN DEE: Now, your Majesty, shall one King rise up against another, and there shall be bloodshed throughout the whole world. Fighting between the devil, his kingdom, and the kingdom of light.

8.

VIV, ANGEL and SPHINX arrive at VIV's live/work studio. All very minimalist – a black box. Nothing but a mattress on the floor.

VIV: Man, I was glad to get out of there. Once those two start kicking off…

SPHINX: Don't worry about it.

VIV: Well, I do worry. They're not wrong, you know. I might not like how they go about it but I can't help admiring them. The intensity of that anger. We should be angry. Why aren't we all that angry all the time?

ANGEL: It's exhausting!

SPHINX: Nice place you got here.

VIV: I can't believe I've never brought you here before. This is it! This is where it all happens.

VIV sits on the edge of her mattress and starts skinning up.

ANGEL: It's very…minimalist, isn't it.

SPHINX: She's got a bed. What more do you need?

ANGEL: I just wasn't expecting it to be so…black.

VIV: I've always felt happy surrounded by black. When I was a kid I used to say to my mum, What if there was a colour darker than black? She'd say, there isn't, darling, nothing's darker than black. And I'd say, but if there was a colour darker than black, I'd paint my whole room in that colour. And then I'd paint the windowsills black. To cheer the place up a bit.

ANGEL: Yeah but you're an artist! I thought there'd be pictures all over the walls and old paint in saucers and little mannequins and stuff.

VIV: I'm not that sort of artist.

SPHINX: Course she's not…What sort of artist are you then?

VIV: I do live art.

ANGEL: Like people watch you paint?

VIV: No! Like, performance. Like performance art.

ANGEL: Oh.

SPHINX: Like those fucking Yodas down Covent Garden.

VIV: Not exactly.

SPHINX: So what then? What do you do all day in your black minimalist abode?

VIV: Well, I make performances.

ANGEL: You don't make any actual…things?

VIV: No. I don't like things. I started out making things. That's what I trained in. As a kid I made stuff all the time. Model dinosaurs. You name it.

ANGEL: So what happened?

VIV: I don't know. There are enough things. Don't you think? You think about all the giant shopping malls and all the landfill and…I don't want to add to it. We have enough things.

SPHINX: So what do you use to make your performances?

VIV: Not much. Just my body, really. That's my ideal. Just rock up. No things. No stuff. No clothes, mostly.

ANGEL: Nice.

VIV: Not the way I do it, sunshine.

SPHINX: Course not.

VIV: I've got a gig coming up. You should come down and see.

SPHINX: Yeah.

ANGEL: Yeah, good, yeah. – So can anybody be a live artist?

SPHINX: Cos I'm alive.

ANGEL: Me too.

SPHINX: Barely.

VIV: I think you're both artists already.

SPHINX: Piss artists.

VIV: No, seriously. Anarchists and queers and punks and, you know. Even someone like Mad. If you think of her as just some, you know, twisted fire-starter, she's a pain in the neck. Think of her as an artist, she's brilliant.

ANGEL: Don't fucking tell her that.

SPHINX: Nah, she'll want a fucking grant.

VIV: People who change things. Dangerous people, who tear things up and let the energy out. That's art. If you want to know what I make: I want to make change.

SPHINX: *(Pulling off his shirt and falling back on the mattress.)...* Spare change, more like.

9.

Music plays at H.Q.

BOD is parading up and down in her crown, humming to herself. AMYL is working on her MacBook. CRABS and KID are in bed together, watching YouTube videos on KID's phone, the sound competing with the record that's playing. MAD is bored, drunk, reading Hit-Girl again or some other comic book.

AMYL suddenly loses patience.

AMYL: Oh absolutely fuck this.

MAD: What's your problem? *(She puts down the comic book and gets out her phone.)*

AMYL: I can't concentrate. This place does my head in sometimes.

BOD: I really think this suits me.

AMYL: Give us a break, Bod.

BOD: It's not everyone who can pull off a crown. Maybe I can convert it into a crash helmet?

CRABS: That would be distinctive. You should have nicked some pearls while you were at it.

BOD: I don't like pearls.

AMYL: No, pearls are for the pure, thank you very much.

CRABS: That's your problem, Amyl. All pearls and no oyster.

AMYL: Fuck you. What's that you're watching?

CRABS: I don't know. Something on YouTube. *(To KID.)* What are we watching, hon?

KID: It's Happy Days.

AMYL: What, like with Fonzie?

CRABS: No, it's a band.

KID: A singer. Happy Days. That's the singer.

CRABS: He's kind of cute.

KID: I know him a bit. His brother lives on my estate.

CRABS: I like, I like.

They watch some more. BOD is exasperated.

BOD: I don't believe this. I thought this generation was all about activism. There's nothing active about any of you! The world's going to end and no one will notice. They'll all just be hypnotised by their glowing screens. I should just chuck everyone's phone in the river. Then maybe you wouldn't be such fucking boring company!

MAD: *(Still looking at her phone.)* If you're bored, go join the EDL. I hear their numbers are down.

BOD's phone starts to ring.

BOD: Oh thank fuck! *(Looking at the screen.)* Unknown Caller to the rescue! *(Answering the phone.)* Hello?…Hello? What? Who is this?

CRABS: Most people would hang up. She's just hanging on.

AMYL: For dear life.

BOD: What's that? When? – Yes, of course, I'd love to.

MAD: Who is it?

AMYL: God, I expect.

BOD: Near enough. It's Borgia Ginz's assistant. Borgia wants my opinion on his latest signing.

MAD: You're not going, are you?

BOD: Of course!

AMYL: Ha! They all fall in the end.

MAD: She's never had any principles to begin with.

KID: *(To CRABS.)* Hey, I thought you were going to introduce me to Borgia Ginz?

CRABS: Oh, I don't give up my contacts just like that. You need to convince me you're worth it first.

KID laughs and they kiss.

KID: I'll trade you. Happy Days for Borgia Ginz.

BOD: I'd better get ready.

BOD goes off to get changed.

AMYL: Well. If she goes down to *those* woods today, she's sure of a big surprise... *(Laughs.)*

10.

QUEEN ELIZABETH, watching it all from above. ARIEL listens, below.

ELIZABETH: As a child I was told a story of the sun, and of the Labyrinth which guards a sacred city. This Labyrinth is built of crystal and mirrors, which reflect and refract the sunlight into a myriad of sparks and rainbows, in which the unwary victim is lost forever.

In the centre of the Labyrinth is a deep blue lake, where an old poet keeps watch over the goldfish.

It is said that, before the division of light and darkness, Helios invaded the sacred city, attracted by the great beauty of the virgin Queen who ruled it. But, lost in the maze of mirrors, the young sun god was maddened by his

29

own burning reflections, until finally he stumbled blind from the Labyrinth and dived into the blue lake; and the colourless fish who swam the lake were dyed gold; and the young god's rays imprinted themselves on earth, and from that time forth, man discovered gold where the sun had cast his shadow.

To us, the world is such a Labyrinth. If we should enter it without the thread of knowledge, all is lost and wasted. Wary must we be of such refractions as sow confusion.

11.

BORGIA GINZ, Emperor of Mediocrity, makes an entrance – something he really knows how to do. BOD awaits him, and they embrace extravagantly.

BOD: Borgia!

BORGIA: Baby!

BOD: Understated as ever.

BORGIA: It's just the way God made me, babe. – Oh who am I kidding? God had nothing to do with it. You know, there are only two human-made artefacts visible from space: the Great Wall of China, and me.

BOD: I don't know how you do it.

BORGIA: Ha! You wanna know my story, babe? It's easy. This is the generation who grew up and forgot to live their lives. They were so busy watching my infinite livestream. It's all about the power, babe. It's not what you make, it's what you own that counts. Without progress life would be unbearable. Progress has taken the place of heaven! These kids have no sense of reality. Just screens. I own their world of buffering phantoms.

You name it, Bod, I snapped them all up. BBC, CNN, MTV, HBO, BFI, FBI, WTO, NHS, SWP, DWP, DUP... I bought them all and rearranged the alphabet. Without me, none of it exists.

BOD: So who's this latest addition to your stable?

BORGIA: Ah yes! I thought you should see this. It might be of interest. Lights please!

It's showtime – and out walks AMYL NITRATE, looking like a fucked-up animatronic effigy of Britannia.

BOD: Fuck me, it's Amyl Nitrate!

BORGIA: She's going to Make Eurovision Great Again! Hashtag: #MEGA. She'll be number one all over the world.

AMYL mimes to a souped-up version of 'Rule Britannia', goosestepping across the stage. It's like Nigel Farage's wettest ever dream, Brexit remixed as loveless burlesque. The sounds of war and football crowds drench the soundtrack.

BORGIA is rapt; BOD is appalled but fascinated.

As the routine gets underway, CRABS arrives back at H.Q. with HAPPY DAYS in tow, both of them off their faces, and they start to undress each other. Some excitement but not much romance.

12.

CRABS and HAPPY DAYS are fucking in pink polythene sheets.

MAD is filming them on her phone.

CRABS: *(To MAD.)* He's cute, isn't he? Kid showed me him on YouTube and I got her to introduce us.

HAPPY DAYS: *(Referring to MAD.)* Does she have to do that?

MAD: Yes.

HAPPY DAYS: Really?

MAD: 'For the comfort and safety of all our customers, your sad lonely fuck may be recorded for quality control purposes.'

HAPPY DAYS: Fucking surveillance everywhere.

CRABS: She just likes to watch. Ignore her. I don't mind.

BOD arrives back from BORGIA's studio. She takes off her clothes, puts on the crown, gets a bowl of Cheerios.

MAD: Say your name for the camera.

HAPPY DAYS: Fuck right off.

MAD: Fuck Write-Off? That's a nice name. Suits you. Where are you from, pickle?

HAPPY DAYS: Chelsea. World's End.

BOD: Oh we're all from World's End now, mate. Crabs do you have to keep bringing your waifs and strays back here? You can practically smell the chlamydia on this one.

HAPPY DAYS: Yeah you can fuck off and all.

BOD: Such charisma!

CRABS: Who cares about charisma? He's got a fantastic arse.

MAD: Hey, Happy Shopper, how does it feel to be a sex object?

HAPPY DAYS: Fucking love it mate.

MAD: Yeah?

HAPPY DAYS: You should try it sometime.

CRABS: Hey! No getting distracted. Leave him alone, Mad! He's more fun than a vibrator.

BOD: And only slightly less intelligent. Honestly, Crabs, I don't know what you see in these clapped-out straight guys.

MAD: Give you a clue. *(Gestures.)*

CRABS: Oh come on. It's hardly the crime of the century.

MAD: No, babe, it's much worse than that.

HAPPY DAYS: Ahhh, I think I'm going to come!

BOD: Hey, not yet! You fucking hit and run merchant! You
don't come until she's come. That's the rules round here.
No jizzing till we give you permission. Or we'll fucking
finish you off once and for all. Right, Mad?

CRABS: Anyway, Mad's not ready for your close-up yet.

BOD: Ugh! I can't stand it. Porn and Cheerios isn't a good mix.
I'm going to be sick.

BOD gets up and walks away.

HAPPY DAYS: Too late, I'm coming!

MAD: Right!

*Still filming on her phone, MAD pounces on the mattress and pulls
the polythene over HAPPY DAYS's face. CRABS is just as excited
by this turn of events and she joins in happily as the two of them
suffocate HAPPY DAYS.*

BOD: We don't like the likes of you around here. This is
supposed to be a safe space.

MAD: So we're going to have to make you safe now, treacle.

HAPPY DAYS: Oh fucking hell!

MAD: There you go. Just like that. The perfect money shot!
And...Fade to black.

HAPPY DAYS expires beneath the polythene.

BOD: Is he dead?

MAD: Dunno. He's a straight white cis bloke. How can you
tell?

They all laugh – CRABS despite herself.

MAD: Yeah no he's dead. He's really most sincerely dead.

CRABS: Fuck.

MAD: What?

CRABS: I feel sad now.

BOD: Ugh.

CRABS: I do! Just for a moment I thought he might be the one.

MAD sniggers.

CRABS: You can laugh but I really did.

BOD: Jesus, Crabs, where's your head at?

MAD: Your mind's totally fucked from all that *Twilight Saga* crap you watch.

CRABS: Why are you all against me?

BOD: We're not! We're trying to save you from yourself.

CRABS: No but. Just for a moment I fell in love with him.

BOD: Love is an incredibly bourgeois heteronormative concept.

CRABS: I know.

MAD: Sometimes I think your entire existence is just some cheesy nostalgia-fest love song.

CRABS: Better that than being a psycho pyromaniac.

BOD: Come on, ladies, no bickering. Let's get this dead fucker out of here.

They hastily wrap the naked corpse of HAPPY DAYS in polythene and start to drag him away.

Music plays: The Ink Spots: 'I Don't Want To Set the World on Fire'

13.

VIV, ANGEL and SPHINX lie tangled up together naked in her bed.

ANGEL joins in with the Ink Spots song; it fades and only his surprisingly pure voice continues.

VIV: *(To SPHINX.)* Your brother's got a beautiful voice, hasn't he?

SPHINX: Yeah…Nice dick too.

ANGEL: Hey! Don't objectify me…Oh go on then.

They laugh; then a moment's easy silence.

ANGEL: Nah, it's your time now, Viv. Time for the women to take over once and for all. Fuck equality. The men need to take a seat. We've had the run of it much too long.

SPHINX: Oh nice! He hands it all over to you just as we've terminally fucked it all. 'Here you go! There's no hope by the way!' Isn't that friendly?

VIV: To be fair, we were always terminally fucked. As soon as capitalism was invented. The very first time one monkey stole a banana off a smaller monkey, we were fucked. It was just a matter of how long it would take to all play out.

SPHINX: That's cheerful.

VIV: Doesn't mean I'm not optimistic. All the time there's any creativity in people, there's hope. All the time we're capable of noticing that it's now, there's reason for hope.

ANGEL: What's now?

VIV: Now. The present. That's why I make the work I make. That's why I do performance. It only exists in the present. We have to keep putting ourselves back in the present. That way there's no fear, there's no resentment. There's just us. There's just the question of us. Who we are. Who we're going to be.

Silence.

ANGEL: *(To SPHINX.)* I love you, brother.

SPHINX: Yeah. I love you too.

VIV: And I love both of you.

SPHINX: It's good, innit.

VIV: You two. You've really got things sorted, haven't you?

ANGEL: Well, you're right though. All we've got is now. And here. And each other. Life's short. The world's brutal. We're all fucked. But this is perfect.

VIV: Yes it is.

VIV gets out of bed, and stands naked in the light streaming in through the window.

VIV: Come on. It's a nice day. Let's go out.

ANGEL: Aw, do we have to?

VIV: Where do you boys want to go?

SPHINX: I know. Let's go and visit Max.

14.

QUEEN ELIZABETH and JOHN DEE in the royal box.

ELIZABETH: John Dee, this place hath a desolate forboding.

JOHN DEE: The eyes of man are blinded.
Here are all the flowers of springtime,
all riot of colour and sweet scent.
The honeysuckle entwines the rose,
her sweetness ravished by bees.
Here all is in harmony.

ELIZABETH: Of this harmony see I but little.
Here all is stones and wasteland.

JOHN DEE: The eyes of men are weak
The circle they compass is small.

The eyes of angels are strong
They compass the known stars.
Here where the winds meet
Dwells he who tends the garden.
In his eyes are the words:
Silence is golden.

15.

AMYL is writing her History. MAD appears, suddenly naked, as if out of nowhere, holding a sheet of paper triumphantly.

MAD: Amyl! Amyl, I wrote you something.

AMYL: Babe. I'm kind of in the middle of something.

MAD: It's for your History book. Let me read it to you…
(Clears her throat.) 'Chapter Five. The Birth of Empire. It all began in the Renaissance, when the original Queen Lizzie and her gang of Imperialist thug advisors began sending ships out on Naval expeditions across the seven seas.

When these explorers struck land they claimed, with the special arrogance you only get from cis white men, that they had discovered the country that indigenous people had been living on for thousands of years.

After that, Lizzie 1.0 and her warmongering cronies sent out more ships to help civilise the dark and savage regions of the world. And so, to the shores of West Africa, South Asia and the Americas came the first ever white saviours, with a Bible in one hand and a gun in the other. Bringing the word of God and a fuckload of plastic cutlery to swap for the natives' gold, their land, their freedom. It's the little things.

Four hundred years later there's no shortage of nostalgia for the good old days when Britannia ruled the waves. We're constantly reminded of our Great Bloody Empire in the fabric of our cities and our monuments, our schools and our tv shows. But despite these constant reminders, privately educated white men still spend all day arguing on the internet about whether racism exists. While lucky Asma thanks the stars of neoliberal colonialism as she sweats over her sewing machine on her 80p an hour wage in eastern Bangladesh.'

AMYL: …That's not bad actually! I'd probably focus less on the Lizzie shit…

MAD takes a lighter to the piece of paper she has written the history on. It instantly goes up in flames and vanishes.

Mad! What the fuck are you doing?

MAD: Setting it right. You gotta write it down. Burn it up. Start again!

MAD runs off laughing, leaving AMYL behind. AMYL collects herself.

All right. Quiz time. What jubilee is it?

Come on. 1977 was silver. 2002 was fifty years, that's gold. Sixty years was diamond. What's sixty-five?

Uranium. I looked it up. It's the Queen's uranium jubilee. True.

Sixty-six is snowglobes. Sixty-seven is mephedrone. Sixty-eight is poltergeists. Sixty-nine is Pop Tarts and, if she still hasn't pegged out by then, seventy is the password to ████ █████'s laptop.

You know what? Try as I might, I just can't hate the Queen. I haven't got it in me. There's too much else. I mean she's just so fantastically beside the point. She's like a turd that won't flush. A jewelled turd. That's exactly the figurehead this fucking down-the-pan country deserves.

At this point, history has fuck all to do with kings and queens. At least, the way I'm going to write it.

16.

CRABS and KID are outside BORGIA's studio, waiting to go in and see the great man.

KID: Oh... I don't fancy this now.

CRABS: You nervous?

KID: Course I'm nervous. I'm bricking it.

CRABS: You don't need to be. You have natural talent oozing out of every pore. Anyone can see that. – Come on, you were the one who wanted to meet Borgia Ginz. And you passed my test...with flying colours. So here we are.

KID: Is he intimidating?

CRABS: Borgia? Hardly. He's a sweetie.

KID: Okay.

CRABS: Just don't get on the wrong side of him, that's all.

KID: I don't like people with a wrong side.

CRABS: You don't mind Mad. She's got like fifteen sides and they're all wrong. Come on. Let's go in.

Inside the studio, BORGIA is sitting with his assistant, SCHMITZER.

SCHMITZER: Mr Ginz, we've just had a preliminary sales report through for the new Lounge Lizard track. It's through the roof, sir. Fifteen million downloads in three days.

BORGIA: Good, Schmitzer, very good. As long as the music's loud enough, we won't hear the world falling apart. *(Laughs uproariously.)*

SCHMITZER: I've just got off the phone with Richard Branson's people, he wants to borrow some more money.

BORGIA: No. Fuck that dumb hippy cunt, I'm so sick of her shit.

SCHMITZER: Yes, sir.

BORGIA: What else?

SCHMITZER: Marina Abramovic called again. She's insisting you cast her in this show when it transfers to London.

BORGIA: Marina? She fucking hates theatre.

SCHMITZER: Yes, I think that's why she's so keen to do this show, sir.

BORGIA: All right. Tell her if she promises not to get her tits out for once, or bleed all over the damn set... she can play you, Schmitzer.

SCHMITZER: ...Very good, sir.

SCHMITZER notices CRABS and KID lurking.

SCHMITZER: Oh, it looks as though Ms Crabs is here to see you, sir.

BORGIA: Excellent. Thank you Schmitzer. – Crabs baby!

SCHMITZER shows CRABS and KID in, and then withdraws.

CRABS: Hi Borgia. I hope we're not interrupting. This is strictly a business visit. I've been doing a little talent scouting for you. I'd like you to meet my friend Kid. She's one hundred per cent sex, darling. I'm going to be her manager.

BORGIA: I see. Well, what can I do for you? Or, more importantly, what can you do for me?

BORGIA leers at KID.

KID: Hello, Mr Ginz.

BORGIA: Ha! Very good. Did Crabs teach you that?

CRABS: She's a natural. She's going to be the next Justin Bieber.

BORGIA: Oh, a jumped-up drug-addled lesbian, you mean? How thrilling. I'm sorry, I'm concentrating all my energies just for the moment on Lounge Lizard. It turns out there's a lot of money to be made selling basic genderfuckery to ten-year-olds.

CRABS: Kid's way better than Lounge Lizard. Aren't you? She's totally authentic. With the right support she'll make five times the money. I guarantee it.

BORGIA: ...Well there's no harm in auditioning you I suppose.

KID: I don't care about the money. I care about my integrity as an artist.

A beat, then BORGIA bursts out laughing.

CRABS: *(Embarrassed.)* She's very young.

17.

VIV, ANGEL and SPHINX arrive at MAX's house. Moustachioed MAX, dressed in Hawaiian shirt, shorts and baseball cap, is tending to his highly idiosyncratic garden – in which all the flowers are plastic.

SPHINX: See? I told you it wasn't far. – *(Calling out.)* Max?

ANGEL: *(Quietly to VIV.)* You're going to love this. Max is proper avant garde.

MAX: Oh, look who it is.

SPHINX: Hello Max.

ANGEL: Hi Max.

SPHINX: This is our friend Viv.

VIV: Hello.

MAX: All right, chicken?

VIV: Nice to meet you.

MAX: Someone obviously hasn't read the memo.

VIV: Sorry?

MAX: Don't be sorry, love, there's more where that came from. Come through, I'm just in the garden.

VIV looks round the garden in disbelief.

ANGEL: See. I told you.

VIV: Wow! Max, this is a very...distinctive garden.

MAX: Thank you very much. Yeah. It had a bad case of weeds a few years back so I sprayed it all with poison. I was in the army for a long time, never got the chance to kill anyone first or last, so when I came out, I killed all the weeds in the garden instead. It looked a bit sad after that so I planted all these plastic flowers.

VIV: It must have been very challenging in the army.

MAX: The army? It's a fucking con is what it is. It's just their way of solving the unemployment problem. You're much more likely to die from boredom than a bullet. Still, I made the best of it. I was on a nice little earner pimping out the boys to the locals in the pub. The army's always seen most of its action in bed. – Ah, no! I think this fake carnation's got mildew.

MAX sprays the flower with an aerosol.

MAX: I mean just think. America and North Korea and who the fuck else, all sitting on a big enough nuclear arsenal to blast the sun out of the sky and no one's prepared to press the fucking button. What a waste! Think what it all costs. I pay my taxes. War's got so big now. You know, like Coldplay. It's just lost all contact with people.

VIV: You don't really want the world dead, do you?

MAX: Course I do! It's so much cleaner. You know my idea of a perfect garden? A field of remembrance poppies. – Fuck, a caterpillar!

MAX picks the bug off the flower and eats it.

VIV: *(Not meaning to.)* Caterpillar!

MAX: Don't worry, love, I'm doing the Atkins.

SPHINX: *(Seeing VIV's reaction to all this.)* Maybe we should be going.

MAX: So soon? You only just got here.

VIV: Busy day.

ANGEL: You should come and see one of Viv's art performances some time.

VIV: I'm going to try and rope these boys into the next one.

MAX: Oh yeah? No offence, love, but that arty bollocks isn't really my scene.

SPHINX: And what would your scene be, Max? Apart from the bus station toilets?

MAX: I'm happier down the bingo, me.

VIV: *(Amiably.)* I didn't know people still played bingo.

MAX: That's 'cos you don't know enough real people. You should get outside your bubble, sweetheart.

SPHINX: All right, well.

ANGEL: Yeah, shall we?

VIV: Nice to meet you.

MAX: You too, chicken. Mind how you go.

MAX watches them go.

MAX: Fucking cunts.

He goes back to watering the plastic plants.

18.

BORGIA's studio.

BORGIA and CRABS look on as KID performs a song. She starts nervously but quickly warms up and by the end she's smashing it.

VIV, ANGEL and SPHINX wander in on their way back from MAX's, to add to the audience.

CRABS, VIV and the BOYS applaud wildly at the end of KID's song. BORGIA is more reserved – it's not immediately obvious what he thinks.

BORGIA: Well. You're the real deal, aren't you? We'd better sign you up. Don't move a muscle until we've drawn up the contract.

> *CRABS is overjoyed. KID seems a bit overwhelmed and unsure.*

BORGIA: The only fly in the ointment is, we'll have to change your name. Kid is not a name. It's much too generic. You'll have to be Something Kid or Kid Something…Nasty Kid? No, you're not nasty, are you? Not yet. Naughty Kid? Hm. You'll grow out of it too fast.

KID: You could just use my real name?

BORGIA: Sssh! Don't interrupt when Daddy's talking. Wait! I have it! *(Laughs.)* I'm. a. fucking. genius.

CRABS: What?

BORGIA: Well now. A little *esprit de* punk always goes down well with the tweenies. They like the prefabricated rebellion and the bright colours.

CRABS: So?

BORGIA: So it's obvious. We'll call you…Kid Vicious. *(Laughs.)* Wait here.

> *BORGIA goes off to set the wheels in motion.*

> *SPHINX comes over to KID, who is packing away her stuff.*

SPHINX: You're really good.

KID: *(Without enthusiasm.)* Thanks.

SPHINX: No, seriously. You're great. Take my advice. Don't go anywhere near Borgia fucking Ginz. The music industry's dead. They don't have a business model that works any more, and they don't know what the fuck to do with art or talent or anything actually creative. You're better off busking and doing your own videos and stuff. Honestly. Borgia Ginz is going to package you up, pitch you wrong, sell you out, and dump you in nine months time. And then you'll be just another ex-wannabe on page seventeen of the Metro.

KID: Cheers.

SPHINX: Seriously. You deserve better than that. Listen. Let's get out of here. Why don't you come along and sing to me and my brother?

To CRABS's fury, SPHINX puts a caring arm around KID and leads her away.

19.

In a corner of H.Q., AMYL, BOD, CRABS and MAD are playing Monopoly.

AMYL rolls the dice and moves her counter.

AMYL: Hells yes Community Chest! *(Picks up and reads the card.)* Second prize in a beauty contest. – Second prize? Fucking cheek!

BOD: Who was first?

MAD: Kevin Spacey. In a gimp mask.

AMYL: Ten pounds from everyone. And hurry up please. This is boring now.

MAD: It's been boring all along.

AMYL: Does anybody want to trade Whitehall for Piccadilly?

CRABS: Yes!

BOD: Don't do it, Crabs!

CRABS: Oh, piss off. Here, Amyl. You can have Piccadilly for free. In fact I'll give you two hundred pounds. And all the trains. And then I'll take you backstage and eat you out. Fuck capitalism. Fuck private ownership. And fuck people who won't fuck!

MAD: And fuck this game. What are we doing? It's the 21st century!

BOD: I was just trying to get everyone off their fucking phones.

MAD: You think this is an improvement? You can buy a house in Whitechapel for thirty quid? Yeah, thanks for the reality check, Bod.

AMYL: You only want to pack it in because I'm winning.

MAD: We're playing Monopoly, Amyl. Nobody's winning in this scenario.

BOD: Well fuck it. *(Kicking the board over.)* If you're not into it, we'll just have to think of something else to do. Is anyone putting the kettle on?

No response. MAD gets her phone out.

BOD: Oh well. You lasted about twenty minutes without your phone. Well done Mad. Very brave…Who knows what might have happened in that time? The world might have come to an end. Donald Trump might have dropped the bomb on North Korea. Paloma Faith might have tweeted a picture of her brunch.

A video starts to play on MAD's phone.

MAD: Oh fuck off!

BOD: Don't you fucking tell me to fuck off.

MAD: I wasn't! I was telling this advert to fuck off. I'm just trying to watch this video. – Skip!

BOD: *(Looking over her shoulder.)* Ugh! Who's that ugly mug?

MAD: That's Lounge Lizard, Bod. The most hyped pop star in the world right now, but of course you wouldn't know about that, because there isn't a Lounge Lizard board game.

BOD: I know all about Lounge Lizard. Borgia Ginz's new hot property. Well, one of them. *(Shooting a look at AMYL, who smiles back.)*

CRABS: They're marketing him to tweenies as some kind of genderqueer icon.

AMYL: Oh please. That's such bullshit.

CRABS: I know.

AMYL: God I'm so sick of these leeches. Hijacking our aesthetic, stealing from our culture, but never for one moment having to live with any of our danger. Yes, very well done, Eddie Redmayne, here's another Oscar nomination for hopping so nimbly out of your motorized wheelchair and into a frock. *So brave.* Meanwhile our trans sisters and brothers can't get jobs, can't get proper healthcare, and oh by the way are being killed on the streets. I am so tired. I'm so tired. I am so fucking over it.

MAD: And on top of all of that – this is a shit song.

BOD: Hmm. Sounds to me like the world wouldn't miss Lounge Lizard if he didn't make it all the way to the end of his fifteen minutes of fame…

Beat.

CRABS: Oh… You're serious!

BOD: *(Getting her flick knife out.)* Well I have to admit: Monopoly was getting a bit dull.

CRABS: Bod you're crazy…I love it! I'll call Schmitzer and find out where Lounge Lizard's staying tonight.

BOD: Come on all of you! Let's go. Come on!

The gang pull themselves together and stumble out.

20.

LOUNGE LIZARD alone in a hotel room, miming along to his own song on headphones. A plain towelling dressing gown hangs on a coathook.

There's a knock at the door. LOUNGE LIZARD doesn't hear it to begin with. Another knock. He takes out his earbuds.

LOUNGE LIZARD: Who is it?

BOD *(Outside.)*: Room service.

LOUNGE LIZARD: All right, come in.

BOD enters, followed by CRABS, MAD – filming the whole thing on her phone, and finally AMYL.

BOD: Mr Lizard, I presume?

LOUNGE LIZARD: Who are you? Wait, I didn't order room service…

BOD: No, I'm your roving reporter, Miss Vengeance. And this *(Gesturing to MAD.)* is our camera person, Miss Recording Angel. You're being livestreamed to the world. I wonder if you might have a few words for your fans, Mr Lizard?

LOUNGE LIZARD: Oh. Well…

BOD: Words such as 'So long'? 'Farewell'? 'Auf Wiedersehen'? 'Goodbye'?

LOUNGE LIZARD: How do you mean, exactly?

BOD: Well you know how avid your fanbase is, Mr Lizard. You know how they hang on your every word. Every shallow thought that passes through your tiny, fraudulent mind. So I thought you might grant them an exclusive interview from the privacy of your own surprisingly modest hotel room?

She runs her fingers over the dressing gown, finally pulling out the cord.

LOUNGE LIZARD: Mr Ginz doesn't like us spending money on extravagances, so... – Sorry, where did you say you were from?

BOD: We're from the future, Mr Lizard. We've come from the future to smash up the present. So maybe you could start by telling your overheated preteen fans –

BOD throws the dressing gown cord around LOUNGE's neck and starts to strangle him.

BOD: – what does it feel like to die? What's that you say, Mr Lizard? Boring? Is it as boring as your hit song? Is it? Is it as boring as your tedious exploitative existence? Great. I bet you're loving every minute of it. You must feel right at home. Oh! Here come your angelic backing singers. – What's that? Heaven's too full? They won't let you in? Fire regulations?

LOUNGE LIZARD gives up struggling as MAD moves in for the moment-of-death close-up. CRABS is on the sofa, reading Vanity Teen and sucking a lollipop. AMYL hangs back, watching coolly.

BOD: Hm! I enjoyed that one. That was a proper buzz. Come on. I need a drink.

The gang start to leave the room as music continues to leak from LOUNGE's earbuds.

21.

ARIEL materialises in the hotel room, followed by QUEEN ELIZABETH and JOHN DEE. The dead body of LOUNGE LIZARD lies on the floor.

ELIZABETH: A great chill embraceth this place.

DEE: Indeed, your Majesty, it's not much better than a Travelodge.

ELIZABETH: What signifieth this death? A dark parable it seems, to my understanding.

DEE: Light and dark, hot or cold, living or dead: mankind is attracted to the polarities.

ARIEL: Consider the world's diversity and worship it. By denying its multiplicity you deny your own true nature. Equality prevails not for the gods' sake, but for people's. Humans are weak and cannot endure their manifold nature.

ELIZABETH: Sweet angel, little I thought to be thus transported from my dear familiar England.

ARIEL: I will be correspondent to command.

What shall I do? say what; what shall I do?

The sound of a gathering storm.

ELIZABETH: Spirit Ariel, we would have knowledge of God. We, Elizabeth of England, a feather in the wind of time, pray for knowledge, in the great whirlwind of shadows on the edge of the abyss. Where is God, friends? Is God dead?

Thunder. Lightning. Interval.

PART 2

22.

AMYL chats to audience members as they return from the interval.

Somewhere in H.Q., a radio plays witteringly. Then, after an inane jingle, M.I.A.'s 'Bad Girls' starts to play.

AMYL: *(Interrupting herself.)* Ah, wait wait wait! I love this song. Do you know this song? I fucking love her so much, she's so beautiful and smart… She wrote this song for me. *(Laughs.)* Definitely! Wait, I'm going to… *(Shouting up to the control box.)* Wait, can you turn this up? – Can you turn it up?

The level on the radio is turned up a bit.

AMYL: No like properly turn it up! Go on!

As the track really drops at the 40s. mark, it explodes into the auditorium.

AMYL lipsyncs to the track, and the whole company (with the exception of the QUEEN, aloft) converges around AMYL – a riot of queer colour, punk disarray and black bloc fierceness. Gradually a tightly choreographed dance routine emerges which draws in equal parts on the 'Bad Girls' video and the famous group dance at the end of Adam & the Ants' 'Prince Charming'.

Towards the very end the group disperses and H.Q. is re-formed.

23.

ANGEL and SPHINX have taken KID up onto the roof. They look out over the desolate city, passing a spliff between them. Distant sirens and occasional gunfire.

KID: Why'd you bring me up here? I've never been on the roof before.

ANGEL smiles and puts his arm around KID.

ANGEL: And then the Devil came unto her and took her to a very high place and he showed her all the boroughs of London. And then the Devil said, 'I'll give you all of this if you'll just go down on your knees.' And she answered, knowing full well that none of it was fit for human habitation: 'Fuck off, Satan.' And Satan left. And an Angel came and ministered unto her.

KID laughs. SPHINX points to a distant tower block.

SPHINX: See that block of flats over there? That's where me and Angel were born. On the fourteenth floor. I don't remember ever seeing the ground till I was four years old. We were just up locked alone with the telly and the Playstation. The first time I saw flowers, I freaked out. Imagine! I was frightened of dandelions! My gran picked one once and I pissed myself. There's nothing that isn't grey. Sight: concrete. Sound: adverts. Touch: plastic. Taste: plastic. No seasons. It's all regulated by thermostat. Strawberries in winter for those that can afford them. It's only just now become obvious to the middle classes: these tower blocks are nothing more than the most efficient mechanism yet designed for killing poor people. Other than war. It's not even that different from war. It's war waged by other means. We're all just casualties. I didn't even know I was dead until I was fifteen. No love, no hate. Not till we got the fuck out.

KID: *(Bursts out laughing.)* You're a real drama queen.

ANGEL laughs; SPHINX laughs reluctantly.

ANGEL: She's onto you! – Come on, time we were going. *(To KID.)* You coming with us?

KID: Where are we going?

ANGEL: You remember our mate Viv? She's doing a performance tonight down The Seal Club.

KID: Oh okay, nice – you're going along to support her.

SPHINX: Support her? Nah mate! We're in the fucking show! Come on!

24.

Back at H.Q. Old-school punk music playing.

AMYL is at her desk, writing her book.

BOD is lying on one of the mattresses; MAD is cutting the word 'LOVE' into her back with a knife.

AMYL: *(Reading aloud.)* 'Chapter Twelve.'

Groans from BOD and MAD.

MAD: Fucking do we have to? Another Cipramil history lesson.

AMYL: 'Chapter. Twelve. On Human Rights.'

BOD: Jesus.

AMYL: 'Human beings, of course, have no rights. It's all a huge fiction. It didn't occur to anyone that they had any rights until various liberal hypocrites decided to just invent them for no reason. First there were political rights, and then there were material rights, and once there were material rights, no one gave a fuck about the political rights any more. The meaning of human rights got distorted by politicians who said there were no rights without responsibilities. In other words, you had to earn your rights, which means they were never rights to begin with. Nowadays people despise human rights, because they can't stand that other people have them, and they despise other people. They'd rather destroy human rights as an idea altogether than admit that the people they hate are actually human. For the liberal hypocrites, this is the end of civilisation as we know it. But civilisation as we know it has always been a fucking disaster for almost everyone, so who gives a shit? We're better off out of it.'

MAD: Finished?

AMYL: Yes thank you.

BOD: That wasn't bad, actually.

AMYL: Too kind.

BOD: *(To MAD.)* Is it finished?

MAD: Yep.

BOD: Go and get the salt.

MAD: Where is it?

BOD: I don't know. On the shelf.

MAD goes off to find the salt.

MAD: Are we going to the Seal Club later to see Viv's performance?

BOD: 'Performance'!

MAD: …She's doing a performance, right?

BOD: Fucking pretentious pile of wank. Art has become such an indulgence. Real people don't care about art. Viv thinks she's so edgy! Course you are, love. Try existing on disability allowance and fucking food banks. That's edgy.

MAD comes back with the salt and starts to sprinkle it over BOD's back. BOD winces.

AMYL: Use food banks a lot yourself, do you Bod?

BOD: Who cares about food? It's just shit-in-waiting. Like Jacob Rees-Mogg.

AMYL: Only you're being seasoned even as we speak. I can do the vinegar if you want.

BOD: Salt in the wound, babes. Just making it permanent. Not like fucking experimental theatre spunking a load of money up the wall for the sake of some middlebrow fiction that immediately disappears. God I hate actors. Why call it acting? It's the opposite of action. Wankers. It's all fucking nostalgia. It's the only way they can get through the day. Avoiding any real action. I'm really pissed off that Sphinx and Angel have let themselves get roped in to Viv's art-wank tonight. –…Did you want to go?

MAD: *(Disappointed.)* Nah it's all right. I'm just going to get fucked up tonight and watch cartoons.

BOD: Jesus, you're as bad as they are.

MAD: I love watching *Adventure Time* when I'm fucked.

BOD: What am I supposed to do?

MAD: You just lie there and bleed, baby. What else is there to do?

BOD: …All right, let's go to the club.

MAD: *(Grins.)* Yay! – At least it won't be boring, Bod.

BOD: It better fucking not be.

25.

The Seal Club: a super-alternative queer club staked out among squatted warehouses in a not-yet-gentrified part of town. This could almost be Berlin in 1981 or Taboo in 1986, with perhaps a whiff of the Shunt Vaults in 2009. Some of the clubbers have really dressed up, some have really dressed down or barely dressed at all; punk meets BDSM meets charity shop New Romantic. Disorienting lights cut through pumped-out smoke. Plenty of dark corners for reckless behaviour of all kinds.

A remix of Minty's 'Useless Man' plays very loud.

ANGEL stands outside the club, trying to drum up business. SPHINX is a bit less enthusiastic.

ANGEL: Save your souls, kids! Come on in to witness the greatest live show on earth! Save your poor genderqueer souls! Welcome to the Seal Club! It's a veritable palace of heavenly delights! Tonight featuring performance art!

SPHINX: But don't let that put you off!

Inside, the clubbers dance, kiss, collide and fumble.

BOD, MAD and CRABS are losing themselves in the crowd.

KID looks on delightedly at this whole new world; so too, from above, does QUEEN ELIZABETH.

CRABS is hitting on someone picked apparently at random on the dancefloor – with one eye always on KID, who she's evidently trying to make jealous. But KID is mostly oblivious.

BOD and MAD are dancing together. MAD is off her face on something and really letting herself go.

MAD: *(Shouting to be heard above the music.)* See, you're glad we came now, aren't you?…I'd forgotten how much I like this place!

BOD: What? I can't hear you!

MAD: *(Louder.)* I said, I'd forgotten how much I like this place!

BOD: *(Louder.)* And I'm saying I can't hear you! *(Gesturing to herself as if to say: 'Have you forgotten I'm deaf?'.)*

Beat. BOD laughs and pulls MAD towards her, and they start making out.

CRABS: *(To the clubber she's hitting on.)* I absolutely fucking love your look. It's so…you. You're very you. I think that's amazing.

Up in the royal box, QUEEN ELIZABETH is transfixed. We hear her thoughts in v/o:

ELIZABETH: O, wonder!
How many goodly creatures are there here!
How beauteous humankind is! O brave new world,
That has such people in't!

Then spoken live:

ELIZABETH: Fuck yeah!

She laughs wildly.

The music fades as the club compere approaches the mic.

COMPERE: All right, you lot. Looking gorgeous this evening. Like you always do. You never let me down!

Much whooping.

COMPERE: So we've got a real treat for you tonight. A live artist who's really making a name for herself, and you're about to find out why. Please give a massive Seal Club welcome to the incredible... Viva!

The crowd goes wild.

Music: a sulphurous electro version of 'Jerusalem'.

VIV emerges, naked, covered in clay, miming to an aria from Stainer's Crucifixion.

She's followed by ANGEL and SPHINX. ANGEL wears a leather jacket, a white t-shirt, no pants, big black boots, and a Skeletor mask; he carries a Bible. SPHINX is naked except for similar boots and a mask of Michelangelo's David.

The boys wind barbed wire around VIV's body. They perform their (somewhat) rehearsed gyrations.

VIV stops the music for a moment to elicit a barbaric yawp from the crowd, who go wild.

VIV and the boys pull the other clubbers up onto the stage one by one and they all dance together euphorically. A picture of how it all could be.

As she tries to get to a better place to see from, KID is jostled by another clubber and a scuffle breaks out. She gives as good as she gets, but it's all over very quickly.

BOD and MAD aren't into the art. They decide to go back to H.Q., and slip out.

CRABS is making some progress with the person she's been hitting on.

The act finishes. VIV and the boys get down off the stage and go and get cleaned up and (at least a bit) dressed.

Two uniformed cops come into the club and start mooching around. CRABS doesn't notice: she only has eyes for her new friend. KID does notice, and is visibly wary, but she's waiting for ANGEL and SPHINX to come back.

CRABS: Oh my god that was so good. Weren't they incredible? They're friends of mine – well the boys are. But I've never seen them do anything like that before. Who knew they were so talented? I mean I knew they had special qualities… Well as you could see. *(Laughs.)* But I mean I think I have an eye for talent. I'm a performer myself, so… Devising mostly… It's where you… Doesn't matter. Doesn't matter. You know, you are just so authentic. It's amazing.

One of the COPS approaches CRABS and her friend.

CRABS: *(To the COP.)* And so are you! The uniform looks so great on you, hon. Especially in this light. You almost look like actual filth.

1ST COP: Special Branch, miss.

CRABS: Miss! Ooh, you can stay. And just how special is your branch?

She reaches for his crotch and he grabs her wrist to stop her.

1ST COP: I'm a police officer, madam. I'm investigating reports of subversive activity in this establishment.

CRABS: Oh! You should have been here five minutes ago, darling, it was all kicking off on stage. *(She mimes a bit of the action.)*

1ST COP: You've obviously had a refreshing evening out, miss. If I were you I'd have the good sense to leave it there and head home.

The penny finally drops with CRABS that this really is a police officer.

CRABS: …Yes, officer, that sounds very wise. I could do with some air anyway. *(To the clubber.)* You coming?…You don't speak any English, do you?…All right, well. It's been lovely meeting you all but I'm suddenly craving a hellride on the night bus and a nice lukewarm falafel. Toodles.

As CRABS slips away, the boys emerge back into the main area of the club, where they meet with KID. VIV follows a bit behind them, carrying three bottles of beer, which she distributes when she catches up with them.

KID: That was so cool!

ANGEL: Did you like it?

KID: That blows my mind that you would just stand up and do that in public!

SPHINX: Well it's only what we'd be doing at home anyway if we weren't here.

KID: That's what I mean though! It's one thing doing it in private…

VIV: But that's one of the things I really want my work to destroy. You know? It's so obvious that there's a direct link between the privatisation of the NHS and, and, and air traffic control and that whole privatising agenda, and the ways in which privacy's become the defining feature of our whole social fabric. We don't share anything any more, we don't hold anything in common, we're all in our little private rooms and that's what makes us fearful of each other. That's what they exploit. My work's going, fuck my privacy, and fuck yours.

The other COP starts to sidle over.

VIV: Anyway. Cheers! – *(To KID.)* Mate, I'm sorry, I didn't think to get you one.

KID, who has clocked the police officer, gestures not to worry about it. She's trying to indicate to them that the COP is approaching. Eventually she breaks away from the group a bit. The COP follows.

2ND COP: *(To KID.)* Past your bedtime, isn't it, son?

KID: Son?!

VIV: Er, excuse me…

2ND COP: *(Still to KID.)* Oh I do beg your pardon. *Miss.* What's a nice girl like you doing hanging around with a gang of nasty scumbags like this?

ANGEL: I don't know what she's doing, but I'm just waiting for you to suck my dick.

SPHINX: Yeah, come on, sexy. Let's make bacon!

ANGEL blows a kiss at the COP.

Without warning the COP pulls out a gun and shoots ANGEL and SPHINX. They both fall dead to the floor.

An abrupt silence – a kind of freeze frame while we hear ARIEL in v/o, with music:

ARIEL: Eternal weaver of the universe
    great fisher of stars
    neither circle without line
    nor line without point
    thus the world is made
    in the horizon of eternity
    the pearl in the eye of creation
    the peacock's tail unfurls
    wrapped in the sun's shadows
    in it all colour is distinguished:
    blue it is, and saffron
    blue of the flowers of Delos
    black it is, and violet
    black, blacker than the raven
    in it are the emeralds of venus
    and the white of the raging seas.

The world of the club starts to thaw out again.

VIV: Oh fuck –

KID: Fucking hell!

KID makes a break for it and escapes into the night. The COPS follow in pursuit.

The clubbers all scarper, leaving behind VIV, rooted to the spot in shock and disbelief.

26.

The COPS chase KID over the rooftops.

27.

Back at H.Q.

MAD and AMYL are having an old-school fencing duel on the stairs. BOD looks on dispassionately.

MAD: No more history for you, Amyl! Just histor-ectomy!

She lunges at AMYL.

AMYL: Ow! Fuck.

BOD: Need any help there, Amyl?

AMYL: No thank you. I've got through life perfectly fine with brains and a pair of fists.

MAD: Fists?! I can take someone out with a hard stare, mate.

AMYL: Well, smell you, Poundshop Medusa!

BOD: All right, enough with the Dogtanian shit. Try these for size.

BOD throws two sets of boxing gloves at AMYL and MAD.

MAD: Nice! Come on then. Let's go.

AMYL: You're on.

BOD: In the red white and blue corner, we have Miss Amyl Nitrate. In the black corner with scorch marks all over it, we have Mad Medusa. And may the worst girl win.

The two of them start to fight.

VIV arrives back at H.Q., utterly traumatised. She sits in BOD's chair. At first, nobody notices. Then:

BOD: Hey! Art school Messiah! What are you doing sitting in my chair?

VIV: I… Sorry, I didn't…

MAD: What's wrong, Viv?

VIV: Something…terrible's just…

BOD: What?

VIV: Down at the Club. After you left, these two cops came in. With guns. I don't know… They shot the boys. Sphinx and Angel. They're dead.

Stunned silence for a moment. Then:

MAD: What about Kid?

VIV: What?

MAD: Kid was with you, wasn't she?

VIV: Yes, I…I don't know what happened. She got away.

MAD: So where is she?

VIV: I'm sorry, I don't know. She's very smart, though. She knows the streets better than anyone. She's fast. She'll be okay. I'm sure she will.

28.

KID has hidden in a builders' yard. As the COPS round the corner, KID makes a break for it, but they corner her. The 2ND COP smahes a bottle against the wall.

2ND COP: Oh princess. See, this is what happens when you fall in with a bad crowd. Another promising young life cut short. The story writes itself, doesn't it? Bad luck.

The two COPS attack. KID screams.

We don't see any more.

29.

H.Q. again, a few minutes later.

VIV is still very distraught. BOD pours her a large vodka in a 'Fuck Everything and Become a Pirate' mug.

BOD: Come on. Drink this. A toast for Angel. And then another one for Sphinx. Come on, no crying. Crying doesn't change anything. It's a waste of time. I'm making fire bombs if you want to help.

VIV looks at her, alarmed.

BOD: We'll get the bastards. I swear.

MAD: Yeah we will. It's party time. *(Flicking her lighter.)* We're going to liberate the zoo.

30.

A bar in Shoreditch. They're playing shitty punk covers by Nouvelle Vague.

CRABS is on her own, drinking a cocktail, reading a book.

A man we now recognize as 2ND COP comes in to the bar. Off duty now, out of his uniform and heading home.

COP: What's that you're reading?

CRABS: *(Showing him.)* Žižek. *Violence.*

COP: *(Raising an eyebrow.)* What's it about?

CRABS: *(Not unkindly.)* Take a wild guess.

COP: That was the joke, princess.

CRABS: Oh.

COP: Doesn't look like your sort of thing.

CRABS: No?

COP: No.

CRABS: What's my sort of thing?

COP: I don't know. *Teen Vogue.*

CRABS: As if... I mean, sometimes. *Teen Vogue*'s super political these days. Ugh it drives me mad. The way men don't think you might be capable of reading fashion magazines *and* critical theory. I'm a complex person.

COP: I'm sure you are.

CRABS: And actually only a man would have the cheek to come up to a woman on her own in a bar and comment on what they're reading.

COP: Fair do's. Except: look me in the eye and tell me you're not reading that book specifically so some Man will come over and ask you what it is.

CRABS: Bog off.

COP: You're not even really reading it, are you?

CRABS: Yes I bloody am!...Slowly.

COP: What's he saying then?

CRABS: Dunno. – That violence isn't always where you think it is. Like, things that look violent aren't always. That lots of the worst violence is invisible.

COP: You mean people do it when they can't be seen? That sounds about right.

CRABS: No, but that there's violence in the system. And we don't see it, sometimes. We just see people reacting to it violently and we say they started it. Like they're irrational.

COP: People *are* irrational. They're...scum.

CRABS: I don't think so. I think people do their best.

COP: I can tell you for a fact they fucking don't.

Beat. The COP laughs.

COP: How's your night been?

CRABS: Weird. As usual. How about you?

COP: Yeah, I'd go with weird.

CRABS: What were you up to?

COP: I was down this gay club.

CRABS: Oh!

COP: ...Nah, I'm not! That's why I'm not averse to hanging around an establishment like that. Full of queers and trannies and all that. I go from a seven to a nine just like that.

CRABS: Wow.

COP: What?

CRABS: You're a fucking dinosaur, mate.

Beat. The COP smiles.

CRABS: What?

COP: I'm messing with you. I was down there for work.

CRABS: Oh yeah? What's work?

COP: Work's where you show up somewhere and you have to do some things and they give you money for it.

CRABS: Clever boy. I mean what work do you do?

COP: ...Police officer.

CRABS: Oh...Must be intense.

COP: Some nights.

Silence for a moment.

CRABS: So you've finished your shift for the night?

COP: Yeah. Just popped in for a quick beer on the way home. Get rid of some of the tension, you know?

CRABS: Well, if you're heading back…

COP: Yeah?

CRABS: I could always walk you to your door. Make sure you get home safely.

31.

The other COP stumbles through the concrete wasteland, drinking a beer. The distant sound of gunfire.

AMYL and MAD discover the COP. They creep up behind him and AMYL blinds him with a spray of her perfume.

AMYL: Cefiro from Floris. Not all the good things have disappeared.

MAD: Where's the razor, Amyl? Give me the razor. I'm going to fucking castrate him!

MAD attacks the COP. AMYL helps to hold him. The COP screams, drops to the floor, and tries to crawl away.

MAD: Go on then! Crawl! You fucking bastard! Look at you now! Look at him crawl!

MAD attacks the COP again and this time he is killed.

MAD breaks down and starts to cry. Terrible, desolate wailing.

After a bit, AMYL helps MAD to her feet and leads her away.

32.

QUEEN ELIZABETH, still watching, aloft.

ELIZABETH: The swallow has risen in the east
He rises silently and steals the light of the moon

He washes his hands in the sun
and combs the golden rays of his hair.
His smile brings colour to the morning
He steps forth, he steps forth
Like the leopard in the shade of the oleander.
Ah, the wheel turns; in his hands
The roses of ecstasy burn
The ashes are upon his brow
The waters of Lethe steal upon the golden-eyed.
He dances into silence
and colour deserts the world.

33.

Back at the COP's house. He and CRABS are in bed together. It's the morning after the night before. The COP wakes to find CRABS propped up on an elbow, watching him.

CRABS: Morning, sleepy head.

COP: …Morning.

CRABS: I've been thinking.

COP: …What?

CRABS: Let's get married.

COP: *(Beat; then, sarcastically.)* Sure. Why not. We could have kids.

CRABS: Lots of boys, just like you. I've been wanting to settle down. I think I might have fallen in love with you.

COP: …Okay…Okay. – Not being funny, but do I know your name?

CRABS: My name's Crabs.

COP: Pleased to meet you, Crabs. I'm just called '2nd Cop'.

CRABS: Suits you.

COP: And what did you say you do for a living?

CRABS: Oh, I wouldn't call it a living. I'm an actress. I think I'm supposed to be cool and say 'actor' but when I was a little girl I wanted to be an actress so that's what I am.

COP: Would I have seen you in anything?

CRABS: I mostly do devising.

COP: Right. Well...

The doorbell rings.

COP: *(Saved by the bell.)* I'll get it.

CRABS: Ha!

The COP puts on a shabby dressing gown and goes to the front door.

BOD is standing a few steps back from the door with a Molotov cocktail in her hand.

She grins, holds up the bottle and a lighter; flicks the lighter.

BOD: *(Shouts.)* No future!!

The scene abruptly changes:

34.

AMYL addresses the audience.

AMYL: It's funny, isn't it? In 1977, someone shouting NO FUTURE sounded like the most extreme nihilistic punk. Forty years on, it's a fact. It's mainstream climate science.

In a way it all looks like a massive self-fulfilling prophecy. If you were fifteen when *Never Mind the Bollocks* came out, you're fifty-five now. You're the generation that's been running the planet over the past decade. I mean you look at the world and that's the only explanation that makes sense. The nihilists won. They're in the Oval Office. They're negotiating Brexit. They're sitting round boardroom tables looking at flipcharts that say SHAREHOLDER VALUE and BRAND SYNERGY.

They're running the councils and writing the editorials and recommissioning Ant and Dec.

What we're living through, it's their dream come true.

And I don't necessarily think they're wrong.

Look at where we are. What do we know?

Capitalism doesn't work. Communism doesn't work. Centrism doesn't work. Neoliberalism doesn't work. Globalisation doesn't work. Localism doesn't work. Federalism doesn't work. Social democracy doesn't work. Libertarianism doesn't work. Anarchosyndicalism might work except people are cunts.

Religion doesn't work. Heterosexuality doesn't work. Homonormativity doesn't work. Nuclear families don't work. Gender doesn't work. Medicalisation doesn't work. Morality doesn't work. Postmodernism doesn't work. Narrative doesn't work. Mindfulness doesn't fucking work. Industry doesn't work. Empire doesn't work. Race doesn't work. Slavery doesn't work, so please stop trying to rebrand it. Borders don't work. Free movement doesn't work. Free markets don't work. Freedom doesn't work.

What works?

What works?

Apocalypse works.

I mean yes some porn works and dogs in fancy dress mostly work and despite what you've heard the drugs *do* work and I hope we can all agree that Beyonce works.

But nothing succeeds like apocalypse.

This is not a pessimistic viewpoint. It's where you get to if you follow the logic that all of history points towards. Civilisations fall. It's what they're for.

Burn the lot. Voluntary extinction. It's coming anyway so we might as well press the accelerator. Hasten the end and make room for the next thing.

It's all right.

Some of us already live it, every day. For some of us, apocalypse happened a long time ago, and we're just the cockroaches it left behind.

Bring it on, love. Who gives a fuck.

AMYL walks away in disgust.

CRABS appears at the top of the stairs. She mounts the stair rail and walks slowly, precariously, but with surpassing and surprising elegance, down the bannister.

She dismounts, picks out a posh-looking black dress, and changes into it as she addresses the audience.

CRABS: Sometimes I think you just have to look around at the situation you find yourself in, and go, yeah, this has got a bit out of hand.

Luckily I was pretty unscathed by Bod's firebomb, but even so. Between us we'd killed two cops and two pop singers. Angel and Sphinx and poor Kid were all dead. It was like, this is not good.

It would have been an ideal time to be keeping a bit of a low profile, only Amyl's version of 'Rule Britannia' had gone straight in at number one, so what could we do?

In the end I called Borgia and explained the situation. And he said:

BORGIA appears.

BORGIA: I know just the thing. I have a little place in the country. Dorset.

CRABS: You have a house in Dorset?

BORGIA: No, I own Dorset. That's why it's safe there. We'll go. All five of us. It'll be wondrous.

CRABS: – And so that's what we did. We were driven down to Dorset in Borgia's limousine. The car pulled up at this stately home like something out of Julian Fellowes' deathbed wank fantasy.

BORGIA: I bought it from a couple of clapped out aristos. *Old* money. The costs of upkeep were crippling them. They practically begged me to take it off their hands. Take a look around. It's Access All Areas for you girls. You know there's still a safari park here. You never know what you'll come across in the grounds.

CRABS: True enough. And that was how it came about that Amyl met a rhinoceros.

AMYL, in a fur coat and red boots, confronts a RHINOCEROS.

They stare each other out.

CRABS: There isn't really a story to it. There was just a rhinoceros. And Amyl. She wanted to take a picture. She said it would be perfect for her album cover.

The encounter between AMYL and the RHINO feels strange, but oddly beautiful.

So there we all were. And the strangest thing happened.

We were happy.

A huge table laid up for a banquet arrives in the theatre.

BOD, MAD and BORGIA are wheeled in at the same time.

BOD is dressed in uncharacteristic sports-casual gear, and MAD, equally unexpectedly, in leopardskin. BORGIA is resplendent in a white dress and blonde pigtails. CRABS is in her little black number, and AMYL now slips off her fur coat to reveal a Union Jack dress underneath. You might almost describe the five of them as, respectively, sporty, scary, baby, posh, and, er, ginger...

They are attended by two immaculately smart WAITERS.

The banquet is in full flow. Gaiety! Party poppers! Everyone is tipsy and full of laughter.

AMYL: Borgia, darling. You know how you were saying it's all about power?

BORGIA: Mmm… That sounds like something I'd say.

AMYL: So would you be very sweet and buy me a tank? I need to outdo all those bitches in their 4x4's on the Kings Road.

BOD: And when she finally goes postal and deliberately drives at a bunch of pedestrians, at least she'll do some proper damage.

BORGIA: Of course, darling! Amyl can have whatever she wants. She's my special number one, I'm going to make millions out of her. *(Laughs.)* They all sell out in the end, one way or another. They all get sucked into the machine and it turns them into effigies! Cartoons! It's priceless! They'll be advertising Cu-Cu-Cu-Country Life butter by the end of next year. We may have lost Lounge Lizard in unfortunate circumstances, but now we've gained…The Spliced Girls! Maddy…Bod…Crabs…and Amyl – and of course, I'm the baby of the group! Somebody give me a tambourine! *(Laughs.)* Now look! High time we had a song. You should be singing for your supper. So what's it going to be?

The intro to the Spliced Girls' version of Toyah's 'I Want To Be Free'.

MAD takes the first verse.

We see QUEEN ELIZABETH watching from the royal box, accompanied by ARIEL. She gestures to be taken downstairs to join the party, and so ARIEL accompanies her.

The company assembles around MAD and ELIZABETH, who, united across time, lead them in singing 'I Want To Be Free' together. Banners containing the hand-daubed lyrics of the chorus are unfurled so that the audience can join in.

'I Want To Be Free'

I'm bored

I don't want to go to school
Don't want to be nobody's fool
I want to be me
I want to be me

I don't want to be sweet and neat
I don't want someone living my life for me
I want to be free

I'm going to turn this world inside out
I'm going to turn suburbia upside down
I'm going to walk the streets, scream and shout
I'm going to crawl through the alleyways, being very loud

I don't want to be told what to wear
As long as you're warm, who cares?
I want to be me
I want to be me

So what if I dye my hair?
I've still got a brain up there
And I'm going to be me
I'm going to be free

I'm going to turn this world inside out
I'm going to turn suburbia upside down
I'm going to walk the streets, scream and shout
I'm going to crawl through the alleyways, being very loud

Tear down the wallpaper, turf out the cat
Tear up the carpet and get rid of that
Blow up the tv, blow up the car
Without these things you don't know where you are
Burn down the Sun, and all magazines
Pull down the abattoirs, all that's obscene
Everything in life should be totally free
We should live and let live, and all live our dreams

I'm going to turn this world inside out
I'm going to turn suburbia upside down
I'm going to pull my hair, scream and shout
I'm going to crawl through the alleyways, being very loud

I'm going to be free

*The song finishes, and the company rapidly disperses, leaving
ELIZABETH and ARIEL standing in the otherwise deserted space
of H.Q.*

35.

Sounds of the seashore.

JOHN DEE arrives to join QUEEN ELIZABETH. ARIEL sits at a remove.

ELIZABETH: All my heart rejoiceth in the roar of the surf on
the shingles. Marvellous sweet music it is to my ears. What
joy there is in the embrace of water and earth.

DEE: Yea, a great elixir is the seashore. Here one can dream of
lands far distant and the earth's treasure.

ELIZABETH: The sea remindeth me of youth. Oh John Dee,
do you remember those days? The whispered secrets at
Oxford like this sweet sea breeze, the codes and counter-
codes, the secret language of flowers.

DEE: I signed myself with rosemary, a true alexipharmic
against your enemies.

ELIZABETH: And I with the celandine. True gold of the new
spring of learning. You were my eyes then as now, with
your celestial geometry. You laid a path through treachery
and opened my prison so that my heart flew like a swallow.

DEE: Sweet majestie, to me you are the celandine as then
before, balm against all melancholy.

ELIZABETH: Ah, but, fuck, I was young then.

ARIEL is at the mic.

ARIEL: There and back.
>There and back.
>The waves break on the shores of England
>The white cliffs stand against the void
>We gaze seaward contemplating the night journey
>The sun sinks lower
>The moon waits to make her entrance
>In the south a picture of wind on the sea
>In the west a vision of silver dew falling into a chalice
>Flowing on a sea of pure gold
>In the east a black hoarfrost
>The sun eclipsed by the wings of the phoenix
>In the north a howling chaos
>into which a black rain falls without ceasing
>Now is the time of departure
>The last streamer that ties us to what is known parts.
>We drift into a sea of storms.

ELIZABETH and DEE walk into the distance, and the black dark engulfs them. We hear ARIEL in v/o:

ARIEL: And now Elizabeth and Dee go along the same great highway, and the light of the air about them seemed somewhat dark, like evening or twilight, and as they walked the phoenix spoke and cried with a loud voice: come away!

The sounds of the seashore slowly, slowly fade.

We hear the run-out groove of the sound effects record: and then that, too, fades.

The End.

By the same author

**The Forest and the Field:
Changing Theatre in a Changing World**
9781849434751

Eve
with Jo Clifford
9781786822697

Men in the Cities
9781783191673

Monkey Bars
9781849434690

The Adventures of Wound Man and Shirley
9781849431804

WWW.OBERONBOOKS.COM

Follow us on www.twitter.com/@oberonbooks
& www.facebook.com/OberonBooksLondon